Intimacy
with God

1386094

ALSO BY CYNTHIA HEALD

Becoming a Woman of Excellence

Loving Your Husband

Loving Your Wife *(with Jack Heald)*

Becoming a Woman of Freedom

Becoming a Woman of Purpose

Abiding in Christ

Becoming a Woman of Prayer

A Woman's Journey to the Heart of God

Becoming a Woman of Grace

When the Father Holds You Close

Becoming a Woman of Faith

Walking Together *(with Jack Heald)*

Intimacy with God

A BIBLE STUDY IN THE PSALMS

REVISED & UPDATED

Cynthia Heald

NavPress

BRINGING TRUTH TO LIFE

P.O. Box 35001, Colorado Springs, Colorado 80935

OUR GUARANTEE TO YOU

We believe so strongly in the message of our books that we are making this quality guarantee to you. If for any reason you are disappointed with the content of this book, return the title page to us with your name and address and we will refund to you the list price of the book. To help us serve you better, please briefly describe why you were disappointed. Mail your refund request to: NavPress, P.O. Box 35002, Colorado Springs, CO 80935.

The Navigators is an international Christian organization. Our mission is to reach, disciple, and equip people to know Christ and to make Him known through successive generations. We envision multitudes of diverse people in the United States and every other nation who have a passionate love for Christ, live a lifestyle of sharing Christ's love, and multiply spiritual laborers among those without Christ.

NavPress is the publishing ministry of The Navigators. NavPress publications help believers learn biblical truth and apply what they learn to their lives and ministries. Our mission is to stimulate spiritual formation among our readers.

ISBN 1-57683-187-6

Cover design by: Jennifer Mahalik
Cover photo by: Michael Keller/ The Stock Market
Creative Team: Kathryn A. Helmers, Terry Behimer, Vickie Howard

Published in association with the literary agency of Alive Communications, Inc., 7680 Goddard Street, Suite 200, Colorado Springs, CO 80920.

Unless otherwise specified, Scripture quotations in this publication are from the *New American Standard Bible* (NASB), copyright © 1960, 1962, 1963, 1968, 1971, 1972, 1973, 1975, 1977. Other versions include: *The New King James Version* (NKJV), copyright © 1979, 1980, 1982, Thomas Nelson, Inc., Publishers; the *Holy Bible International Version®* (NIV®), copyright © 1973, 1978, 1984 by International Bible Society, used by permission of Zondervan Publishing House, all rights reserved; and the *Holy Bible: New Living Translation,* copyright © 1996, used by permission of Tyndale House Publishers, Inc., Wheaton, Illinois 60189; all rights reserved.

1 2 3 4 5 6 7 8 9 10/05 04 03 02 01 00

FOR A FREE CATALOG OF
NAVPRESS BOOKS & BIBLE STUDIES,
CALL 1-800-366-7788 (USA)
OR 1-416-499-4615 (CANADA)

Contents

Preface

The Lord had been encouraging me to study the psalms. To reinforce His desire, He prompted a friend to give me *The Treasury of David*. Charles H. Spurgeon, who wrote and edited this rich commentary on the psalms, declares, "More and more is the conviction forced upon my heart that every man must traverse the territory of the Psalms himself if he would know what a goodly land they are. They flow with milk and honey, but not to strangers; they are only fertile to lovers of their hills and vales. None but the Holy Spirit can give a man the key to the Treasury of David; and even He gives it rather to experience than to study. Happy he who for himself knows the secret of the Psalms."[1] A little reluctantly, I began my pilgrimage into this vast poetical land. Over a period of time, I have listened to, cried with, and learned from these special men of God. I am no longer a stranger, but now I desire to take up long-term residence in their hills and vales.

How much the psalmists have taught me about relating to and being intimate with God. My heart is humbled deep within me, for I have realized how shallow my concept of walking with God has been. Still, I am encouraged, for the psalmists have shown me not only their heart's response in all situations, but they have also meaningfully testified to God's heart in faithfully relating to them. Because of this study, I am motivated to spend the rest of my life pursuing deeper intimacy with God.

Love in Christ,

Cynthia Heald

Cynthia Heald

The Desire for Intimacy

1. Our Longing for Intimacy

2. God's Desire for Us

In the beginning, Adam and Eve enjoyed a very special, deep, intimate relationship with God and each other. "The man and his wife were both naked," we are told, but they were "not ashamed" (Genesis 2:25). Their nakedness symbolized their freedom and confidence in God's love for them and their acceptance of and trust in each other.

After the tragic intrusion of Satan and his deception, Adam and Eve hid themselves from the presence of the Lord. Their close fellowship with God was irrevocably broken. Dan Allender writes that Adam's nakedness referred to "his awareness of being utterly exposed as helpless and contemptible."[1] Adam himself told God, "I heard Your voice in the garden, and I was afraid because I was naked; and I hid myself" (Genesis 3:10, NKJV).

As it was in the beginning, so it is now. We find ourselves still wanting to hide from God, yet also wanting to answer Him when He calls, "Where are you?" Dare we move away from among the trees? Despite our fear and shame, we sense our need not only for reconciliation, but for restoration to that original intimate relationship with our heavenly Father. For there is within each of us a longing for love and intimacy that only He can fulfill.

But God gave the most precious gift of His Son to take our sin upon Himself on the cross so that we might be reconciled to our Father. When we accept Him, He clothes us in His righteousness so that we can draw near with confidence to the throne of grace. In Christ, we are secure and free in our standing before God. We can step out from whatever trees of fear may surround us. We are no longer bound by the belief that if we tell God how we really feel or what we think, God will judge us or cause some disaster to come upon us.

This is true intimacy: confidence that what we reveal about ourselves will be understood and that the One to whom we disclose ourselves will accept us, seek our good, and communicate support and love.

But practically, how do we deepen our friendship with God? Who has gone before us to show us the way? In their honesty, vulnerability, and revelations of the heart, the psalmists demonstrate to us how to relate to God intimately. Studying and meditating on the Psalms will give us courage to open our hearts to our Creator as we realize His great desire for us.

Our
for Longing
Intimacy

Whom have I in heaven but You?
And there is none upon earth that I desire besides You.

PSALM 73:25 (NKJV)

—————

Can we find a friend so faithful,
Who will all our sorrows share?
Jesus knows our every weakness—
Take it to the Lord in prayer.[1]

—————

Come near to the holy men and women of the past and you will soon feel the heat of their desire after God. They mourned for Him, they prayed and wrestled and sought for Him day and night, in season and out, and when they had found Him the finding was all the sweeter for the long seeking.[2]

—A. W. TOZER

There is a restlessness deep within each of us that compels us to search for the person, the place, the job, the "god" that will fill the void and give us peace. This restlessness drives us to find someone who will love us for who we are, understand our fears and anxieties, affirm our worth, and call our lives into account. To admit our need for and dependence upon God requires humility and vulnerability, which paves the way not only for knowing God, but also for becoming intimate with Him. "Mutual love and confidence are the keys to intimacy," writes J. Oswald Sanders; "deepening intimacy with God is the outcome of *deep desire*." [3] May this prayer of David's become our own:

Hear my cry, O God;
Give heed to my prayer.
From the end of the earth
I call to Thee, when my heart is faint;
Lead me to the rock that is higher than I.
For Thou hast been a refuge for me,
A tower of strength against the enemy.
Let me dwell in Thy tent forever;
Let me take refuge in the shelter of Thy wings.

PSALM 61:1-4

A CRY OF LONGING

1. The heartfelt longing of the psalmist is beautifully expressed in Psalms 62, 63, and 73. Read through these prayers and write down any key words and phrases that communicate an intense desire for intimacy with God.

[Concerning Psalm 73] His God would not fail him, either as a protection or a joy. His heart would be kept up by divine love, and filled eternally with divine glory. After having been driven far out to sea, Asaph casts anchor in the old port. We shall do well to follow his example. There is nothing desirable save God; let us, then, desire only him. All other things must pass away; let our hearts abide in him, who alone abideth for ever.[4]

—CHARLES H. SPURGEON

2. Choose one of these psalms that you feel provides a vivid portrait of longing to read in greater depth. In what ways can you identify with the psalmist's need for closeness with God?

3. Look for the descriptions of God in these three psalms. What evidences can you find of the psalmist's knowledge and experience of God—that is, what is his view of God?

4. How would you describe the person who acknowledges his or her need for God, in contrast to the one who is restlessly searching for intimacy?

5. As you look at your own life, what do you think are the "gods" with which you try to fill the void that can be satisfied only by intimacy with God?

If we have a godly thirst, it will appear by diligence in frequenting the place and means of grace; brute beasts for want of water will break through hedges, and grace-thirsty souls will make their ways through all encumbrances to come where they may have satisfaction.[5]

— THOMAS PIERSON

Author's Reflection

In 1985 a friend lovingly cross-stitched Psalm 73:25-26 for me because she knew this was my favorite passage. For many years now these words have hung on a prominent place on the wall above my desk as a constant reminder that my desire should be only for the Lord. In Psalm 73, Asaph questioned God's care for the righteous. As he observed the prosperity of the wicked, he felt slighted and mistreated! Then he went into the sanctuary of God and received an eternal perspective on life. He realized that to desire the world and to scoff at God leads to a slippery path that can result in destruction. To revel in riches can only be temporary, but to desire God is to begin to understand that only the eternal can satisfy. His conclusion is found in the beautiful verses declaring that God is enough. I have learned from Asaph that the more I admit my need for intimacy with the Lord, the more I desire Him; the more I desire Him, the deeper my intimacy.

Your Longing for Intimacy

6. Select a favorite passage (two to four verses) from your reading in this chapter that expresses your longing for intimacy.

   a. Write it out here in your preferred Bible version. In the coming week, read this passage each day and meditate on it whenever you have a few spare moments. Committing it to memory will help imprint its truth on your mind and heart.

   b. Tell the Lord in the form of a short written prayer why this passage is significant to you, or how your desire for Him has been kindled by the readings in this chapter.

Great as He is He loves His children to be bold with Him.[6]
— Charles H. Spurgeon

Other Scriptures on our longing for intimacy
Isaiah 26:9; Philippians 3:7-11

2
God's Desire for Us

When You said, "Seek My face,"
My heart said to You, "Your face, LORD, I will seek."

PSALM 27:8 (NKJV)

There's the wonder of sunset at evening,
The wonder of sunrise I see;
But the wonder of wonders that thrills my soul
Is the wonder that God loves me.[1]

What matters supremely, therefore, is not, in the last analysis, the fact that I know God, but the larger fact which underlies it — the fact that He knows me. I am graven on the palms of His hands; I am never out of His mind. All my knowledge of Him depends on His sustained initiative in knowing me. I know Him because He first knew me and continues to know me.[2]

—J. I. PACKER

"Amazing love! How can it be, that Thou, my God, shouldst die for me!" This great hymn by Charles Wesley conveys the wonder of God's desire to have fellowship with us. The God who created us has not abandoned us to grope blindly through life. He has provided, at great expense, all that we need for life and godliness. God is our *personal* Creator, and He wants to be our Shepherd who protects and provides for us. He has proclaimed His love for us, and He waits only for our response.

Many, O LORD my God, are Your wonderful works
Which You have done;
And Your thoughts toward us
Cannot be recounted to You in order;
If I would declare and speak of them,
They are more than can be numbered.

PSALM 40:5 (NKJV)

GOD LONGS FOR INTIMACY

1. God's longing for His children is communicated in Psalms 8, 23, 27, and 139. As you read through them, write down the key thoughts and phrases that express God's desire for us.

2. How would you describe the psalmist's responses to God's care?

---

3. What specific assurances does the psalmist affirm about God's involvement in his emotions and experiences?

4. What do the psalmist's observations of God's activity reveal about God's nature and character?

If, then, you feel not your soul mightily affected with the condescension of God, say thus unto your souls, "What aileth thee, O my soul, that thou are no more affected with the goodness of God? . . ." Oh the condescension of his love to visit me, to sue unto me, to wait upon me, to be acquainted with me?[4]

Author's Reflection

It wasn't until I was a parent that I began to realize God's desire to be intimate with His children. Spiritually I was born into God's family, just as my children were physically born into our family. But it is not enough just to bear children; a loving parent has a great desire to have a vital relationship, a bond of intimacy with his or her child. In a small way, I understand God's desire to be lovingly involved with and close to us, just as I love and want to be near my children.

God is well acquainted with our ways; He has laid His hand upon us. His thoughts toward us are precious. He is our Shepherd, who asks us to "seek His face." He is our Savior, whose desire for intimacy is ultimately manifested in the Cross. He is our loving Father, who has adopted us so that He can be intimate with us. God does long to be with His children.

GOD'S DESIRE FOR YOU

5. Select a favorite passage from your reading in this chapter that expresses God's longing for His people.

   a. Write it out, at the top of the next page, in your preferred Bible version. In the coming week, read this passage each day and meditate on it whenever you have a few spare moments. Committing it to memory will help imprint its truth on your mind and heart.

(Write your answer here)

b. Offer to the Lord in a short written prayer your response to this revelation of who God is.

In God there is no hunger that needs to be filled, only plenteousness that desires to give. . . . God who needs nothing, loves into existence wholly superfluous creatures in order that He may love and perfect them.[5]

—C. S. Lewis

Other Scriptures on God's desire for us
Jeremiah 24:7; Matthew 11:25-30; Revelation 21:2-4

The
Creator,
a Worthy
Confidant

Intimacy connotes familiarity and closeness. It involves our deepest nature, and it is marked by a warm friendship developed through long association. In order for us to become intimate with another, we must find in him a true confidant—one in whom we can safely confide our secrets.

What are the characteristics of such a true friend? Most of us look for someone we respect as wise and just; one we can trust implicitly; one we feel safe and secure with; one who will respond to us, help us in the right way, and be available whenever we want to share. True confidants are rare, and fortunate are those who have one.

There is One who meets these criteria perfectly: the Keeper of souls who never sleeps, who calls us into fellowship—"Call to Me, and I will answer you, and I will tell you great and mighty things, which you do not know" (Jeremiah 33:3). The marvelous affirmation of the psalmists is that the Creator of the vast universe is also our intimate Confidant.

3
God
Is
Righteous

Righteousness and justice are the foundation of Your throne;
Mercy and truth go before Your face.
Blessed are the people who know the joyful sound!
They walk, O LORD, in the light of Your countenance.

PSALM 89:14-15 (NKJV)

———— ɷɷ ————

My hope is built on nothing less
Than Jesus' blood and righteousness;
I dare not trust the sweetest frame,
But wholly lean on Jesus' name.[1]

———— ɷɷ ————

Our Father, we love Thee for Thy justice. We acknowledge that Thy judg-ments are true and righteous altogether. Thy justice upholds the order of the universe and guarantees the safety of all who put their trust in Thee. We live because Thou art just—and merciful. Holy, holy, holy, Lord God Almighty, righteous in all Thy ways and holy in all Thy works. Amen.[2]

—A. W. TOZER

It is comforting to know that God is righteous. *Righteousness* essentially means "meeting the standards of what is right and just." Righteousness involves goodness, uprightness, integrity, morality, and purity. Righteous means right! Sinclair Ferguson expounds further by asking the question, "But what of the righteousness of God? The idea behind the biblical word *righteousness* is probably 'conformity to a norm.' Given that norm, righteousness is the situation in which things are what they ought to be. In the Old Testament, righteousness is associated with God's covenant. He is faithful to it; in relation to His promise, God always does what He ought to do, namely, fulfill His promise. That is why His righteousness can be expressed in judgment, or in salvation." [3]

But as for me, I will hope continually,
And will praise Thee yet more and more.
My mouth shall tell of Thy righteousness,
And of Thy salvation all day long;
For I do not know the sum of them.
I will come with the mighty deeds of the Lord GOD;
I will make mention of Thy righteousness, Thine alone.

PSALM 71:14-16

HOW GOD DEALS WITH HIS PEOPLE

1. The psalmists proclaim God's justice in Psalms 9, 71, 103, and 109. As you read through them, write down the ways in which God's righteous character was revealed in how He dealt with His people's obedience or rebellion.

2. Choose one of these psalms to read in greater depth. What conclusions did the psalmist reach about God's character?

He will declare or pronounce judgment; he will execute the office of judge. To all people; to the nations of the earth . . . and the declaration is, that in his dealings with dwellers on the earth he will be guided by the strictest principles of justice. . . . He will not be influenced by partiality; he will show no favouritism; he will not be bribed. He will do exact justice to all.[4]

—ALBERT BARNES

3. How did the psalmist's comprehension of God's righteousness affect his life? Look for specific evidence of how this understanding made a difference.

4. In Psalm 109, David personally pleads for God's righteousness on his behalf. How does this psalm encourage you to bring your hurts before God, asking Him to fight for you and freeing you from seeking justice on your own?

We survive in the way of faith not because we have extraordinary stamina but because God is righteous. Christian discipleship is a process of paying more and more attention to God's righteousness and less and less attention to our own; finding the meaning of our lives not by probing our moods and motives and morals but by believing God's will and purposes; making a map of the faithfulness of God, not charting the rise and fall of our enthusiasms. It is out of such a reality that we acquire perseverance.[5]

— EUGENE PETERSON

Author's Reflection

Psalm 109 is unique in its bold expression of David's implicit confidence in God's righteous judgment of his enemy. Charles Spurgeon provides a helpful commentary on the apparent harshness of this psalm: "A psalm of David. Not therefore the ravings of a malicious misanthrope, or the execrations of a hot, revengeful spirit. David would not smite the man who sought his blood, he frequently forgave those who treated him shamefully; and therefore these words cannot be read in a bitter, revengeful sense, for that would be foreign to the character of the son of Jesse. The imprecatory sentences before us were penned by one who with all his courage in battle was a man of music and of tender heart, and they were meant to be addressed to God in the form of a Psalm, and therefore they cannot possibly have been meant to be mere angry cursing."[6]

This psalm encourages me with David's trust in God's ability to "execute righteousness and justice for all who are oppressed." He is depending on God to avenge him. David is not returning evil for evil, but allowing God to justly deal with this man who has betrayed him. Because David understood God's righteousness, he could freely call upon the Lord. So when I come to God hurt, confused, or angry, I too can speak openly, knowing that no matter what I say, God will respond righteously. I cannot persuade God to justify me if I am to blame in any way, nor can I influence Him to punish my enemy unjustly. This opens up great freedom in prayer. God sifts through my feelings and "causes" and either confronts or consoles me in righteousness and justice. He is the perfect confidant.

YOUR RELIANCE ON GOD'S RIGHTEOUSNESS

5. From your reading in this chapter, select a favorite passage that affirms the righteousness of God.

   a. Write it out here in your preferred Bible version. In the coming week, read this passage each day and meditate on it whenever you have a few spare moments. Committing it to memory will help imprint its truth on your mind and heart.

   b. Tell the Lord in the form of a short written prayer how you desire to rely on His righteousness.

Let the words of my mouth—what I say—and the meditation of my heart—what I think—be the kind of words and thoughts that have sat under the judgment of your work, Father, reflecting the instruction, the light and the love of your heart, so that what I am, both inside and outside, will be acceptable before you.[7]

— RAY STEDMAN

Other Scriptures on God's righteousness
Nehemiah 9:7-8; 2 Thessalonians 1:5-8

Is God Trustworthy 4

Our fathers trusted in You;
They trusted, and You delivered them.
They cried to You, and were delivered;
They trusted in You, and were not ashamed.

PSALM 22:4-5 (NKJV)

———∞———

'Tis so sweet to trust in Jesus,
Just to take Him at His word,
Just to rest upon His promise,
Just to know, "Thus saith the Lord."[1]

———∞———

Be assured, if you walk with Him and look to Him and expect help from Him, He will never fail you. As an older brother who has known the Lord for forty-four years, who writes this, says to you for your encouragement that He has never failed him. In the greatest difficulties, in the heaviest trials, in the deepest poverty and necessities, He has never failed me; but because I was enabled by His grace to trust Him He has always appeared for my help. I delight in speaking well of His name.[2]

—GEORGE MUELLER

The young girl sitting across from me cried softly, "I'm afraid that if I trust God, I'll experience some cosmic disillusionment." How can we confidently believe that God is reliable, dependable, and committed to our care? How do we know that if we give Him our lives and reveal to Him our deepest desires, some tragedy will not befall us?

The psalmists who have gone before us can help answer our questions. So much depends on knowing God's character, understanding His past performance, and seeing life from His viewpoint. In Psalm 84:11 we read, "No good thing does He withhold from those who walk uprightly." Sir Richard Baker comments, "But how is this true, when God oftentimes withholds riches and honours and health of body from men, though they walk ever so uprightly; we may therefore know that honours and riches and bodily strength are none of God's good things; . . . and the good things of God are chiefly peace of conscience and joy in the Holy Ghost in this life; fruition of God's presence, and vision of His blessed face in the next, and these good things God never bestows upon the wicked, and never withholds from the godly."[3]

Trust would not be trust if it did not require some commitment from us to walk by faith and not by sight. God is a trustworthy confidant, for He constantly seeks our good.

Blessed be the LORD,
Because He has heard the voice of my supplication.
The LORD is my strength and my shield;
My heart trusts in Him, and I am helped;
Therefore my heart exults,
And with my song I shall thank Him.

PSALM 28:6-7

Choosing to Trust

1. The psalmists had a deep and abiding confidence in the trustworthiness of God. Read through Psalms 31, 40, 55, and 56. Describe the circumstances that prompted the writer to trust in God.

2. David struggled with enemies and rejection. What are your most difficult areas in trusting God?

[Concerning Psalm 56, verses 3-4] It is a blessed fear which drives us to trust. Unregenerate fear drives from God, gracious fear drives to Him. If I fear man I have only to trust God, and I have the best antidote. To trust when there is no cause for fear, is but the name of faith, but to be reliant upon God when occasions for alarm are abundant and pressing, is the conquering faith of God's elect. Though the verse is in the form of a resolve, it became a fact in David's life; let us make it so in ours. Whether the fear arise from without or within, from past, present, or future, from temporals or spirituals, from men or devils, let us maintain faith, and we shall soon recover courage.[4]

—CHARLES H. SPURGEON

3. Summarize the reasons the psalmist cited for trusting God.

4. What other aspects of the psalmist's life were touched because of his trust in God?

Nothing is more difficult, when we see our faith derided by the whole world, than to direct our speech to God only, and to rest satisfied with this testimony which our conscience gives us, THAT HE IS OUR GOD. And certainly it is an undoubted proof of genuine faith, when, however sore the assaults by which we are shaken, we hold fast this as a fixed principle, that we are constantly under the protection of God, and can say to him freely, THOU ART MY GOD.[5]

—JOHN CALVIN

Author's Reflection

I have had a few untrustworthy friends in my life. Some violated my trust by sharing our intimate conversations; some seemed to withdraw when I needed help; and some promised to do something but then for various reasons never followed through. It is rare to find a trustworthy confidant.

In Psalm 55 David recorded his feelings when he experienced the pain of an untrustworthy friend. One of his trusted counselors had turned on him by staying to support David's son Absalom when he seized his father's throne. This "friend" is believed to have been

Ahithophel. David's heart was anguished by this unfaithfulness from a former close friend: "It is not an enemy who reproaches me." Ahithophel was David's equal. They had taken sweet counsel together and worshiped side by side, companions who had made a covenant of friendship. As he reflected on their relationship, David remembered, "His speech was smoother than butter, but his heart was war."

Devastated, David turned to the one and only faithful Friend: "As for me, I shall call upon God"—the true Confidant who never forsakes or disappoints, whose word is always true. After casting his burden on the Lord, David concluded with beautiful words of intimacy: "But I will trust in Thee."

YOUR TRUST IN GOD

5. From your reading in this chapter, select a passage declaring a reason for trusting God.

   a. Write it out here in your preferred Bible version. In the coming week, read this passage each day and meditate on it whenever you have a few spare moments. Committing it to memory will help imprint its truth on your mind and heart.

   b. Tell the Lord in the form of a short written prayer why this reason for trusting Him is significant to you.

It is as if God were saying, "What I am is all that need matter to you, for there lie your hope and your peace. I will do what I will do, and it will all come to light at last, but how I do it is My secret. Trust Me, and be not afraid."[6]

—A. W. TOZER

Other Scriptures on God's trustworthiness
Isaiah 26:4; Jeremiah 17:5-8; 1 Timothy 4:9-10

5
Is a God Refuge

I cried out to You, O LORD:
I said, "You are my refuge,
My portion in the land of the living."

PSALM 142:5 (NKJV)

———ന്ന്ན്———

How often in conflict, when pressed by the foe,
I have fled to my Refuge and breathed out my woe;
How often, when trials like sea billows roll,
Have I hidden in Thee, O Thou Rock of my soul.[1]

———ന്ന്ന്———

He is both *shelter*, offering protection, and *shadow*, offering
refreshment; He offers not only a dwelling place, but, as the verb
abides [Psalm 91:1] indicates, makes Himself our Host and
makes us His protected guests, safe because it is His duty to
make us safe.[2]

A refuge provides protection or shelter from danger or hardship. It is a haven or sanctuary, a place where one may go for help, relief, or escape. Who among us does not seek a secure place away from the daily harassments and stresses of life? There are many false refuges: overinvolvement in recreation or hobbies, hiding in work activities, the single-minded pursuit of possessions, losing oneself in substance abuse. These are our society's primary ways of seeking comfort. But there is only one refuge that offers personal, eternal protection and provision, "a place of quiet rest, near to the heart of God."

For my eyes are toward Thee, O GOD, the Lord;
In Thee I take refuge; do not leave me defenseless.

PSALM 141:8

TAKING REFUGE IN GOD

1. The psalmists who penned the "refuge" psalms 46, 61, 91, and 142 vividly expressed their confidence in God's protection. Read through them, recording the words and phrases used to describe God as a refuge.

2. What are the false refuges in which you tend to seek comfort, instead of turning to God for a safe haven?

The naming of God is done here [Psalm 46:7] with great care. LORD OF HOSTS paints a picture: "hosts" are "armies"—vast, angelic troops, swift and fell, carrying out the divine command. GOD OF JACOB recalls a story: the persistent assailant at the river Jabbok who wrestled Jacob into the intimacy of blessing. A powerful God, "LORD of hosts," and a personal God, "God of Jacob." But there is a surprising reversal in the way these names are connected with our expectations. We expect the military metaphor to be associated with defense, "refuge." We expect the personal metaphor to be connected with intimacy, "with us." But the terms are deliberately rearranged so that we get intimacy with the warrior God and defense from the family friend. A powerful God (LORD of hosts) befriends (is with us); a personal God (God of Jacob) protects (is our refuge).[3]

—EUGENE PETERSON

3. What needs drove the psalmist to seek safety with God?

4. List some of the results or benefits the psalmist experienced because he sought God's protection.

5. If you were a psalmist writing today, what images would you choose to portray God as a refuge?

To take up a general truth and make it our own by personal faith is the highest wisdom. It is but poor comfort to say, "the Lord is a refuge"; but to say He is MY refuge, is the essence of consolation.[4]
—CHARLES H. SPURGEON

Author's Reflection

I usually seek refuge when I am stressed, overwhelmed, or going through a difficult time. I literally want to run away. David expresses my feelings in Psalm 55:6: "That I had wings like a dove! I would fly away and be at rest." I want to go somewhere safe, where I will be given protection and peace. But I only want to be with someone who loves me and is wise enough to provide what I need at the moment.

In Psalm 91, the psalmist announces his decision to make God his refuge. Then he speaks of the Lord's deliverance, protection, and the assurance that he need no longer be afraid. Choosing to abide in the shadow of the Almighty offers the ultimate refuge for any need. This is the choice David makes when he declares in Psalm 27:4 that he wants to dwell in the house of the Lord. In the next verse he explains the reasons behind his desire: "For in the time of trouble He shall hide me in His pavilion; In the secret place of His tabernacle He shall hide me; He shall set me high upon a rock" (NKJV). Here is a sure and secure refuge: hidden in a secret place and set high upon a rock—safe!

It's important to realize that making God our refuge does not keep us from trouble. Rather, it guarantees us that in any affliction, we will not be alone because the Lord is with us. The apostle Paul wrote that he was "hard-pressed on every side, yet not crushed . . . persecuted, but not forsaken" (2 Corinthians 4:8-9, NKJV). How comforting in our agonized world to have God as our "refuge and strength, a very present help in trouble" (Psalm 46:1). This is intimacy when we need it most.

THE LORD IS YOUR REFUGE

6. Select a favorite passage from your reading in this chapter depicting God's safety and protection.

   a. Write it out here in your preferred Bible version. In the coming week, read this passage each day and meditate on it whenever you have a few spare moments. Committing it to memory will help imprint its truth on your mind and heart.

b. Write out a prayer of response to the Lord's offer to be your refuge.

HIS THOUGHTS SAID: Before me continually is the grief of wounds, confusion, suspense, distress. HIS FATHER SAID: Behold, there is a place by ME, and thou shalt stand upon a rock. Then as a frightened child on a storm-swept mountainside would gratefully take his father's hand, and stand on a rock in a place by him, fearing no evil—so it was with the son. For he knew that though the earth be removed and the waters be carried into the midst of the sea, that rock by his Father would never be moved.[5]

—AMY CARMICHAEL

Other Scriptures on God's safety and protection
Deuteronomy 33:27; Hebrews 6:13-20

6

God Is Responsive

I love the LORD, because He hears
My voice and my supplications.
Because He has inclined His ear to me,
Therefore I shall call upon Him as long as I live.

PSALM 116:1-2

———〰———

And Jesus said, "Come to the water, stand by my side;
I know you are thirsty, you won't be denied.
I felt every teardrop when in darkness you cried,
And I strove to remind you that for those tears I died."[1]

———〰———

Inclining the ear is a sign of disposition, even of personal feeling and regard. When we do not care for those who make requests of us, how short and sharp we are with them! When we have personal regard for them, how patiently we listen! How we bend down to attend to them! How we incline our ear! The psalmist read personal interest and affection in that inclining of the Divine ear; and it was precisely fitting that he should respond to love with love.[2]

There are counselors who listen to people bare their anguished souls and then respond by either nodding their heads or asking, "Well, what do you think should be done?" Their counselees eventually leave feeling very frustrated and hopeless.

Not so with God as our confidant. As we learn from this next group of psalms, when the redeemed cry for help, He responds. We will also explore times when it seems that God does not reply. The plaintive song of Heman the Ezrahite (Psalm 88) gives us an example of how a godly person prays when he feels that God is unresponsive. But we are assured that God does incline His ear. Knowing this truth, in faith we can draw close to Him.

In the day when I cried out, You answered me,
And made me bold with strength in my soul.

PSALM 138:3 (NKJV)

THE GOD WHO ANSWERS

1. The psalmists delighted in proclaiming God's goodness in responding to them. Read Psalms 34, 107, 116, and 145 and record the declarations of God's responsiveness.

2. List several ways in which God responded to the psalmist's cry for help.

3. Summarize any conditions you notice that are necessary for God's responding.

4. There are times in our lives when God seems unresponsive. Read Psalm 88, which expresses great longing for God in the midst of one such troubling time. What insights have you gained from your reading in this chapter that would help when God seems to be silent?

Aptly, but dreadfully, the last word of the psalm [88] is *darkness,* and yet therein lies its wonder—the wonder of triumphant faith, that a man should see no light at all but yet go on supplicating in fervent, trustful, ceaseless prayer. . . . What is to be done when the promises of God are denied by the facts of experience? . . . Turn the promises into prayers and plead them before God.[3]

5. How would you summarize the key thoughts concerning God's responsiveness from the psalms you have studied in this chapter?

Author's Reflection

I am not satisfied with a friend or counselor who listens to me but then remains unresponsive to my struggle. If I go to someone to pour out my heart, I want a word, a touch, or some interaction. I certainly cannot be intimate with someone who is distant or apathetic.

I have usually sensed the Lord's listening ear. I have not always had a direct response to my prayers, but His Word assures me that He is always present. It's been said that His silence does not indicate His absence. I know that He inclines His ear to me. When I have not received an immediate answer I know that even if I need simply to wait and trust, I do not wait alone. In my relationship with the Lord, it is necessary that I understand that "no" is a response from God. Perhaps one of my obstacles to understanding God's responsiveness is that He does not always reply when and how I want Him to!

I rely heavily upon the Word of God for faith in the Lord's

responsiveness. We have the testimonies of the psalmists that the Lord hears, saves, delivers, guides, blesses, upholds, satisfies, and preserves His children. One biblical commentator observed, "God is a living Being; in his image we are made; and he is responsive to his children. Contrast the feeling of the heathen, who prays to the stone figure of his god. He can only vaguely fear or vaguely hope, for there is no response from the stone face."[4] Hebrews 13:5 promises, "For He Himself has said, 'I will never leave you nor forsake you'" (NKJV). I may not feel that God has responded, but I have His Word that He is with me. "I love the Lord because He hears my voice and my supplications"—a priceless declaration of intimacy.

GOD'S RESPONSIVENESS TO YOU

6. Select a favorite passage from your reading in this chapter affirming the truth that God responds to us.

   a. Write it out here in your preferred Bible version. In the coming week, read this passage each day and meditate on it whenever you have a few spare moments. Committing it to memory will help imprint its truth on your mind and heart.

   b. In a short written prayer, tell God of your struggles and thanksgivings in recognizing His responsiveness to you.

Think not thou canst sigh a sigh
And thy Maker is not by;
Think not thou canst weep a tear
And thy Maker is not near.[5]

—WILLIAM BLAKE

Other Scriptures on God's responsiveness
Jeremiah 33:3; James 4:8

The Essentials of Intimacy

God is a willing and worthy confidant. But to know Him and enjoy Him in this way involves certain responses on our part.

Fellowship with the Creator demands our respect and reverence for Him as majestic and holy. Jerry Bridges writes, "The fear of God is a heartfelt recognition of the gap between God the Creator and man the creature."[1] Reverence for God is essential in maintaining a proper relationship with Him.

This reverence frees us to be totally vulnerable and honest before God, because as our Creator He knows us fully. The psalmists, confident in God's knowledge of them, are refreshingly truthful. One commentator observed of these honest prayers, "The very presence of such prayers in Scripture is a witness to His understanding. He knows how men speak when they are desperate."[2] Psalm 119, the longest psalm, is a glowing tribute to another essential element of intimacy with God: desire for God's Word. The writer of this psalm had a passion for God and His Word, and his intimacy with God is very evident. One of the major ways of deepening our relationship with our Lord is to know and love His Word.

These next three chapters are important, because they address our responsibility in developing intimacy. Here we will learn what we can do to discover more fully the God who will never allow the righteous to be shaken!

7
Reverence
for God

Friendship with God is reserved for those who reverence him.
With them he shares the secrets of his promises.

PSALM 25:14 (NLT)

———⟋⟋⟍———

O worship the King all glorious above,
And gratefully sing His wonderful love;
Our Shield and Defender, the Ancient of Days,
Pavilioned in splendor and girded with praise.[1]

———⟋⟋⟍———

While we must never on the one hand lose the freedom to enter
boldly and joyfully by faith into God's presence during our lives on
earth, we must also learn how to revere God in our relationship with
Him . . . intimacy cannot occur without respect.[2]

—JOHN WHITE

"Fear and love are the inseparable elements of true religion," wrote A. F. Kirkpatrick. "Fear preserves love from degenerating into presumptuous familiarity; love prevents fear from becoming a servile and cringing dread."[3] True intimacy with God involves not only our love for Him, but also our reverence and respect. The psalmists speak often of fearing God, and of the great blessings bestowed on those who do. Throughout the Psalms we are reminded that by His very nature, God commands our reverence, respect, awe, and fear.

> For great is the LORD, and greatly to be praised;
> He is to be feared above all gods.
> For all the gods of the peoples are idols,
> But the LORD made the heavens.
> Splendor and majesty are before Him,
> Strength and beauty are in His sanctuary.

PSALM 96:4-6

THE FEAR OF THE LORD

1. Psalms 25, 111, 112, and 115 speak of the psalmist's recognition of God's holy character and the importance of fearing Him. As you read through these passages, write down the results in the life of one who reverences God.

2. Why do you think these psalms make a connection between God's holy character and a life rooted in the fear of God?

3. The life described by these psalmists may seem difficult to attain. How does God's responsiveness to those who fear Him provide encouragement for this way of living?

4. How would you describe the difference between mere fearfulness and holy fear?

"Fears the Lord." *Reverence* might be a better word. Awe. The Bible isn't interested in whether we believe in God or not. It assumes that everyone more or less does. What it is interested in is the response we have toward him: Will we let God be as he is, majestic and holy, vast and wondrous, or will we always be trying to whittle him down to the size of our small minds, insist on confining him within the boundaries we are comfortable with, refuse to think of him other than in images that are convenient to our lifestyle?[4]

—EUGENE PETERSON

Author's Reflection

What prompts me to reverence the Lord is the acceptance of who He is—the sovereign Lord of the universe—and the knowledge that someday I will stand in His presence. The Scriptures state that "each one of us shall give account of himself to God" (Romans 14:12). I love the Lord, but I fear Him in the sense that since He created me and called me to Himself through the death of Christ, I am now His child and I will have to answer to Him in regard to how I lived my life. My salvation will not be in question, but the choices I made during my lifetime will be examined. Consequently, I want to live an obedient life for the purpose of bringing glory to God—because He is God!

This is what the psalmist meant when he wrote that the fear of God is the beginning of wisdom. This wisdom gives us understanding that the best life is an obedient life. God's commands are for our benefit, our blessing, our joy. We could not obey if we did not reverence the One who gives the commands.

Fearing God also keeps my intimacy with Him as it should be. In Kirkpatrick's words, "fear preserves love from degenerating into presumptuous familiarity." It is a Father-child relationship. My reverence for God places our intimacy on the highest plane. I do not regard His love or care lightly; it increases my trust, and I do stand in awe of His desire to be intimate with me. "Friendship with the LORD is reserved for those who fear him. With them he shares the secrets of his covenant" (Psalm 25:14, NLT).

Man cannot act wisely if he be his own king, because he is created as a dependent being; and can no more bear fruit by leaning on himself than can the trailing vine. Dependent man must *fear God*. He must cherish the sense of duty; must carry out the designs of his Creator. Practical wisdom is taking our lives to God day by day, and saying, in filial love, to him, "Lord, what wilt thou have me to do?" Life is only ordered aright when God orders it.[5]

YOUR REVERENCE FOR GOD

5. Select a favorite passage from your reading in this chapter regarding the fear of the Lord.

   a. Write it out here in your preferred Bible version. In the coming week, read this passage each day and meditate on it whenever you have a few spare moments. Committing it to memory will help imprint its truth on your mind and heart.

   b. Write out a short prayer expressing your reverence for God.

It is the fear which a child feels toward an honored parent—a fear to offend; it is that which they who have been rescued from destruction feel to the benefactor who nobly and at the sacrifice interposed for their safety—a fear to act unworthily of his kindness: it is that which fills the breast of a pardoned and grateful rebel in the presence of a venerated sovereign at whose throne he is permitted to stand in honor—a fear lest he should ever forget his goodness and give him cause to regret it. Such is the fear of the Christian now: a fear which reverence for majesty, gratitude for mercies, dread of displeasure, desire of approval, and longing for the fellowship of heaven, implies.[6]

—ROBERT NISBET

Other Scriptures on the fear of the Lord
Proverbs 3:7-8; 2 Corinthians 5:10-11

8
Truthfulness with God

LORD, all my desire is before You;
And my sighing is not hidden from You.

PSALM 38:9 (NKJV)

—∞—

Tempted and tried, I need a great Savior,
One who can help my burdens to bear;
I must tell Jesus, I must tell Jesus,
He all my cares and sorrows will share.[1]

—∞—

David emphasized two aspects of prayer: honesty before God, and the fear of God. To "call upon him in truth" simply means "to call on him sincerely." If we want to have revival in our lives, we must begin by being totally honest with God in our praying. But we must not allow this "honesty" to degenerate into undue familiarity; we must "fear him" and show the proper respect and reverence.[2]

—WARREN WIERSBE

I once read a greeting card with the following thoughts written on the front: "Let us live, let us love, let us share the deepest secrets of our souls. . . . " Inside, the card read, "You go first."

How true is this impulse in developing intimacy! We don't want to be the first to bare our souls. God, however, has gone first in our relationship with Him. He initiates, He calls, He provides, He gives—all for us to know Him, to draw near to Him. Once we know and experience God as righteous, trustworthy, responsive, and our refuge, we can begin to feel comfortable with sharing our deepest secrets. David, vulnerable and honest, shows us as no other that it is permissible—even desirable—to "drop our guard" in communing with God.

You know my folly, O God;
My guilt is not hidden from you.

PSALM 69:5 (NIV)

VULNERABILITY WITH GOD

1. Perhaps more than any other writer of Scripture, David models for us how to be honest before God. Read Psalms 35, 51, 74, and 143, and list some aspects of David's life that he shared with the Lord.

The committing of our cause to God is at once our duty, our safety, and our ease.[3]

—ABRAHAM WRIGHT

2. In these psalms, what words or phrases most clearly reveal David's vulnerability before the Lord?

3. David describes various facets of God's character and His responses to His people. Based on these psalms, how would you summarize the truths about God that enabled David to be honest with Him?

4. What encourages you to be truthful with God when you approach Him in prayer?

[Conerning Psalm 51] When the divine message had aroused his dormant conscience and made him see the greatness of his guilt he wrote the Psalm. He had forgotten his Psalmody while he was indulging his flesh, but he returned to his harp when his spiritual nature was awakened, and he poured out his song to the accompaniment of sighs and tears.[4]

—CHARLES H. SPURGEON

Author's Reflection

One of the major lessons I have learned from the Psalms is the freedom I have as God's child to be open and honest with Him. Deep in my soul I feel that some of the thoughts I have shouldn't be verbalized to God — as if He doesn't already know what I am thinking! It is refreshing to read, "Answer me speedily, O Lord, my spirit fails!" "O God, how long will the adversary reproach?" or "Against You, and You only, have I sinned, and done this evil in Your sight." How freeing to speak with the Lord truthfully, to offer my doubts, my fears, and my sin to Him. I marvel at the Lord's patience in letting me wrestle with Him, in letting me pray all that is in my heart.

True intimacy cannot develop unless truth and honesty are at the heart of a relationship. God so desires our closeness that He has recorded in Scripture even the complaints His children have against Him. But it is in the very act of voicing our true feelings that we come to understand the character of our Father. He is righteous, trustworthy, a refuge, responsive, and above all He loves us dearly. God desires that we enjoy His presence, speak sincerely, and cast our burdens upon Him. Who else allows us the privilege of such intimacy?

We do not pray to tell God what he does not know, nor to remind him of things he has forgotten. He already cares for the things we pray about; his attention to them has never flagged from the beginning, and his understanding is unfathomable. He has simply been waiting for us to care about them with him.[5]

—TIM STAFFORD

YOUR HONESTY WITH GOD

5. Select a favorite passage from your reading in this chapter regarding truthfulness with God.

   a. Write it out here in your preferred Bible version. In the coming week, read this passage each day and meditate on it whenever you have a few spare moments. Committing it to memory will help imprint its truth on your mind and heart.

b. Is there some aspect of your life you struggle to bring before God? Using these psalms as examples, write out a brief prayer telling God about your feelings and questions in this area.

Other Scriptures on truthfulness with God
Jeremiah 20:7-18; Luke 22:39-44

9
Love for God's Word

The judgments of the LORD are true;
they are righteous altogether.
They are more desirable than gold,
yes, than much fine gold;
Sweeter also than honey
and the drippings of the honeycomb.

PSALM 19:9-10

———

How firm a foundation, ye saints of the Lord,
Is laid for your faith in His excellent Word!
What more can He say than to you He hath said,
To you who for refuge to Jesus have fled?[1]

———

Heart-fellowship with God is enjoyed through a love of the Word,
which is God's way of communing with the soul by His Spirit.[2]

—CHARLES H. SPURGEON

Some of the titles and descriptions given to Psalm 119 have included "Psalm of the Saints," "The Alphabet of Divine Love," and "The Christian's Golden A-B-C of the Praise, Love, Power, and Use of the Word of God."

The writer of this psalm used three major guidelines in composing it. The first was to address God continually (only four verses do not); the second was to extol the Word of God (only two verses do not mention the Scriptures); the third was to make the psalm an acrostic by using the letters of the Hebrew alphabet to begin each section and verse.

"This sacred ode is a little Bible," exclaimed Charles Spurgeon, "the Scriptures condensed. . . . Oh, that every reader may feel the glow which is poured over the verses as they proceed: he will then begin as a reader, but he will soon bow as a supplicant; his study will become an oratory, and his contemplation will warm into adoration."[3]

May we say with the psalmist,
"I wait for the LORD, my soul does wait,
And in His word do I hope."

PSALM 130:5

LOVE LETTER FOR GOD'S WORD

1. Psalm 119 is the longest psalm in the Bible, but it is also one of the most passionate. Spurgeon wrote of it, "Nor is it long only; for it equally excells in breadth of thought, depth of meaning, and height of fervor."[4] This wonderful psalm is rich indeed! As you read through it, write down the key words and phrases the psalmist used to communicate his love for God's Word.

2. List the synonyms for the Word of God that the psalmist uses most often.

3. What are some of the specific prayers or petitions of the psalmist?

4. How would you describe the ministry, or function, of the Word in the psalmist's life?

5. In what ways can you identify with the psalmist's love for God's Word?

The whole Psalm is animated by a profound inwardness and spirituality, as far removed as possible from the superstitious literalism of a later age. It shows no tendency to substitute mechanical observance of rules for the living application of principles. The close personal relation of the Psalmist to God is one of the most striking features of the Psalms in general, and in few Psalms is it more marked than in this.[5]

—A. F. KIRKPATRICK

Author's Reflection

I love this psalm because it exalts the Word. The psalmist personally describes the sufficiency of Scripture for all of his life—"Your statutes have been my songs in the house of my pilgrimage" (119:54, NKJV). Early in my Christian growth I was taught to cherish, enjoy, memorize, and read the Word daily if at all possible. I am so thankful that I was encouraged to make the Word so much a part of my life. As I have gotten older I have understood that the Scriptures are living and powerful, and that they can discern the thoughts and intents of the heart (Hebrews 4:12). It's been said the Bible is the only book in the world whose author shows up when you open it!

Realizing the power of the Word and that the Holy Spirit, the Author, is present to teach and guide me into all truth, I have a deep passion to abide in the Word: "I have rejoiced in the way of Your testimonies, as much as in all riches" (Psalm 119:14, NKJV). This psalm is an incredible testimony to the power, completeness, and sacredness of this priceless sword of the Spirit.

One of the amazing characteristics of this psalm is that it forms a perfect acrostic. The psalmist has divided the psalm into twenty-two sections corresponding to the twenty-two letters of the Hebrew alphabet, each section representing a different letter of the alphabet. Within each section, every verse begins with that same letter. The psalm writers frequently used acrostics as a memory aid. This psalm is a remarkable example of the psalmist's commitment to detail, another evidence of his intense focus on and devotion to God and His Word. May his passion inflame our hearts with a deepening desire for the wonders of Holy Scripture.

In Matthew Henry's "Account of the Life and Death of His Father, Philip Henry," he says, "Once, pressing the study of the Scriptures, he advised us to take a verse of the Psalm [119] every morning to meditate upon, and so go over the Psalm twice in the year; and that, saith he, will bring you to be in love with all the rest of the Scriptures. He said often, 'All grace grows as love for the Word of God grows.'"[6]

YOUR DESIRE FOR GOD'S WORD

6. Select a favorite passage from your reading in this chapter on love for God's Word.

   a. Write it out here in your preferred Bible version. In the coming week, read this passage each day and meditate on it whenever you have a few spare moments. Committing it to memory will help imprint its truth on your mind and heart.

   b. Following is my effort at expressing my thoughts using the same letter of the alphabet to begin each sentence. Take time to express your desire for God's Word using one or two letters of the alphabet to create a prayer or psalm of a few sentences.

   All of Your words are true, Lord;
   help me to live by them.
   Arouse my heart to love the Scriptures
   so that I will obey them.
   Anoint me with Your Spirit
   that I may understand Your way.

Other Scriptures on God's Word
Deuteronomy 30:8-14; Colossians 3:16

The
Fruit of
Intimacy

True intimacy with God leaves us with a desire for deeper intimacy. The more we know our God, the more we want to know Him. The Creator becomes our confidant, and that is enough. Our thoughts and our voices are lifted in prayer and praise to God and God alone—beautiful evidences of the fruit of intimacy.

10
The Growth of Intimacy

Because he has loved Me, therefore I will deliver him;
I will set him securely on high,
because he has known My name.

PSALM 91:14

———✺———

When peace, like a river, attendeth my way,
When sorrows like sea billows roll—
Whatever my lot, Thou hast taught me to say,
It is well, it is well with my soul.[1]

———✺———

To have found God, to have experienced Him in the intimacy of
our beings, to have lived even for one hour in the fire of His Trinity
and the bliss of His unity clearly makes us say: "Now I understand.
You alone are enough for me."[2]

—CARLO CARRETTO

A young girl was asked to recite Psalm 23 in her Sunday school class. She began by saying, "The Lord is my shepherd; He is all I want." One who is growing in intimacy with God would paraphrase this passage from Psalm 23 in the same way. As we mature in our Christian life, we can begin to say, "Whatever my lot—it is well with my soul." The psalms in this chapter beautifully record the difference that the psalmists' intimate relationship with God made in their lives. What is true for the psalmists can also be true for us.

> What shall I render to the LORD
> For all His benefits toward me?
> I shall lift up the cup of salvation,
> And call upon the name of the LORD.
> I shall pay my vows to the LORD,
> Oh may it be in the presence of all His people.
>
> PSALM 116:12-14

EVIDENCE OF GROWING INTIMACY

1. Psalms 16, 26, 92, and 131 were clearly written in the context of a very close relationship with God. As you read through them, write down the key words and phrases that most clearly reveal the psalmist's intimacy with God.

2. How would you summarize the key changes, or areas of growth, that took place in the psalmist's life as a result of this intimate relationship?

3. What do you notice about how the psalmist's intimacy with God affected his responses toward God and toward others?

4. What changes have you noticed in your own life as a result of pursuing a deeper intimacy with God?

Once the joy of intimacy with God has been experienced, life becomes unbearable without it.[3]

—J. Oswald Sanders

Author's Reflection

Abiding in Christ is the best way I know of developing intimacy. To abide means to continue, dwell, remain, stay. As I consistently take time out of my day to open my Bible and read with a heart to obey, then I will slowly but progressively grow in my relationship with my Father.

A good way to begin time with God is to pray Psalm 119:18— "Open my eyes, that I may see wondrous things from Your law" (NKJV). I think the consistency of meeting with God is really more important than length of time spent with Him. As I have grown in my regularity, though, I find that I desire to sit at His feet a little longer. A Bible reading plan is most helpful in staying as consistent as possible with a busy schedule. Whatever the date, I read that day's Scripture. If I miss several days, I do not try to catch up because I never have enough time to do that.

My life is more than half over, but I feel that I have only begun to fathom the greatness and majesty of the Lord. And the little I have begun to grasp makes me hunger and thirst for more. Perhaps, though, this is the essence of growing intimacy: not being satisfied or complacent, but always desiring to go deeper into the fullness of God.

I do not seek, O Lord, to penetrate Thy depths. I by no means think my intellect equal to them: but I long to understand in some degree Thy truth, which my heart believes and loves. For I do not seek to understand that I may believe; but I believe that I may understand.[4]

—SAINT ANSELM

YOUR GROWING INTIMACY WITH GOD

5. Select a favorite passage from your reading in this chapter that expresses intimacy with God.

   a. Write it out here in your preferred Bible version. In the coming week, read this passage each day and meditate on it whenever you have a few spare moments. Committing it to memory will help imprint its truth on your mind and heart.

   b. Write a brief prayer of thanks to the Lord for His gracious invitation to grow in intimate relationship with Him.

Other Scriptures on intimacy with God
Exodus 33:7-23; John 15:1-17

Praise: 11
The Expression
of
Intimacy

I will sing to the LORD as long as I live;
I will sing praise to my God while I have my being.

PSALM 104:33

———〰———

O for a thousand tongues to sing
My great Redeemer's praise,
The glories of my God and King,
The triumphs of His grace![1]

———〰———

Don't underestimate the value of praise. There is something about
expressing your appreciation to God in words, song, and meditation that solidifies your faith. The Book of Psalms is the Bible's
hymnal of praise. The more you praise God for being who He is—
a loving God who judges righteously—the more you can act upon
your belief of what He is—eternal love.[2]

—JOSH McDOWELL

"Praise should be proportionate to its object," counsels Charles Spurgeon; "therefore let it be infinite when rendered unto the Lord. We cannot praise Him too much, too often, too zealously, too carefully, too joyfully."[3] The Psalms do teach us to praise God much, often, zealously, and joyfully. When our praise seems so inadequate, how encouraging to turn to the Psalms and find the freedom and joy of these hymns to God. It is exciting to begin to exalt God by awakening the dawn with the harp, lyre, and songs of praises to His holy name!

Awake, my glory;
Awake, harp and lyre,
I will awaken the dawn!
I will give thanks to Thee, O Lord, among the peoples;
I will sing praises to Thee among the nations.

PSALM 57:8-9

THE BLESSING OF PRAISE

1. The Psalms are filled with praise for God. Read these expressions of wonder and gratitude in Psalms 67, 96, 148, and 150. Make a list of what the psalmist says about *who* is to praise God and *why* God is to be praised.

2. What do you think motivated the psalmist to encourage praise so strongly?

3. The Hebrew title for the book of Psalms is "book of praises." Many of the psalms were written to be sung as hymns of praise for God's character and deeds. What benefits do you think the people might have gained from singing these remembrances of God's faithfulness to them?

4. What are some expressions of praise that you have woven into your life?

5. What are some specific ways in which you can increase your praise and personal worship of the Lord?

I think we delight to praise what we enjoy because the praise not merely expresses but completes the enjoyment; it is its appointed consummation.[4]

—C. S. LEWIS

Author's Reflection

Praising God has not come naturally to me. Studying praise in the Scriptures has challenged me to increase my praise life and to be more aware of the Creator and His creation. I remember a particular time in my life when I was deeply moved to write a psalm of praise to God. I was on an airplane that had been circling the Denver airport for at least half an hour. Tired and frustrated, I kept staring at the thick cloud cover responsible for our delay. As the plane turned, I was startled to see the most beautiful oranges, yellows, and pinks brilliantly scrolled across the sky. Tears sprang to my eyes as for the first time I witnessed a sunset over the mountains from thirty thousand feet up in the sky. I was so deeply moved by this bold reminder from God that I wrote the following response of praise:

Etched into the sunset,
the signature of God.
In radiant script
He signs
I am.

[Concerning Psalm 150] This noble close of the Psalter rings out one clear note of praise, as the end of all the many moods and experiences recorded in its wonderful sighs and songs. Tears, groans, wailings for sin, meditations on the dark depths of Providence, fainting faith and foiled aspirations, all lead up to this. The Psalm is more than an artistic close of the Psalter; it is a prophecy of the last result of the devout life, and in its unclouded sunniness as well as in its universality, it proclaims the certain end of the weary years for the individual and the world. "Everything that hath breath" shall yet praise Jehovah.[5]

YOUR EXPRESSION OF PRAISE

6. Select a favorite passage from your reading in this chapter that leads you into praising God.

   a. Write it out here in your preferred Bible version. In the coming week, read this passage each day and meditate on it whenever you have a few spare moments. Committing it to memory will help imprint its truth on your mind and heart.

   b. Using one of the psalms from your reading as a guide, write a brief psalm of praise to the Lord.

Other Scriptures on praise
1 Chronicles 29:10-13; Ephesians 5:18-20; Hebrews 13:15;
Revelation 4:1-11

12

A Life of Deepening Intimacy

Show me Your ways, O LORD;
Teach me Your paths.
Lead me in Your truth and teach me,
For You are the God of my salvation;
On You I wait all the day.

PSALM 25:4-5 (NKJV)

———————

Once earthly joy I craved, sought peace and rest;
Now Thee alone I seek, give what is best;
This is all my prayer shall be: More love, O Christ, to Thee,
More love to Thee, more love to Thee![1]

———————

It would seem that admission to the inner circle of deepening intimacy with God is the outcome of *deep desire*. Only those who count such intimacy a prize worth sacrificing anything else for, are likely to attain it. If other intimacies are more desirable to us, we will not gain entry to that circle. . . . The place on Jesus' breast is still vacant, and open to any who are willing to pay the price of deepening intimacy. We are now, and we will be in the future, only as intimate with God as we really choose to be.[2]

—J. OSWALD SANDERS

I watched the flight attendant pull the curtain that separated the first class passengers on the plane from those of us flying coach. That curtain reminded me of the veil used to set apart the Holy of Holies in the Hebrew temple. There were strict rules regarding who was allowed to enter and when, for the Holy of Holies represented intimacy with God.

This temple veil was dramatically torn from top to bottom when Jesus spoke from the cross with His last breath, "It is finished." Now, through Christ, there is immediate access: the privilege and opportunity of intimacy with God is ours at any time.

And yet, as Sanders observed, we are only as close to Jesus as we choose to be. And so the choice is ours—may it be to journey into deeper intimacy with the Lord.

> How blessed is the man who does not walk in the counsel
> of the wicked,
> Nor stand in the path of sinners,
> Nor sit in the seat of scoffers!
> But his delight is in the law of the LORD,
> And in His law he meditates day and night.
>
> PSALM 1:1-2

THE PURSUIT OF INTIMACY

1. The psalmists are our divinely appointed guides for the pursuit of intimacy with God. Read Psalms 5, 61, and 146, and write down the guidance and encouragement you find in them for your own pursuit of God.

2. Choose one of your favorite psalms and explain why it helps you to draw closer to God.

3. Take some time now to reflect on your understanding and experience of intimacy as it has developed through this study. How will the insights you have gained in this study help you grow in your intimacy with God?

God wants you near him and wants lovingly to guide your life. There is still that one clear certainty in an age when nothing else is certain at all: God wants you to be his friend. He wants to give you the pleasure of his company.[3]

—ROGER PALMS

Author's Reflection

If I want to continue to deepen my intimacy with God, then the fulfillment of that desire will take precedence over all other desires. The echo of Asaph's words ring in my ears: "Whom have I in heaven but You? And there is none upon earth that I desire besides You." If that is the cry of my heart, then somehow I will find time to meet faithfully with the Lord. For the very best way of developing deeper intimacy with God is to spend time in His presence. He has given each of us His Word, His Spirit, and a gracious invitation to "Seek My face." Let us respond as did David: "Your face, LORD, I will seek."

Thy Spirit
    quickening my spirit.
Thy thoughts
    renewing mine.
My will
    yielding to Thy will.
My heart
    becoming as Thine.

I want deliberately to encourage this mighty longing after God. The lack of it has brought us to our present low estate. The stiff and wooden quality about our religious lives is a result of our lack of holy desire. Complacency is a deadly foe of all spiritual growth. Acute desire must be present or there will be no manifestation of Christ to His people. He waits to be wanted. Too bad that with many of us He waits so long, so very long, in vain.[4]

—A. W. TOZER

Your Life of Deepening Intimacy

"The end of a matter," wrote Solomon, "is better than its beginning" (Ecclesiastes 7:8). But the end of this study guide can actually be a continuation of a deepening experience of intimacy with God. C. Donald Cole observed, "David was in earnest about praying, so much so that he wrote out his prayers after he had made them."[5] What a good idea! Perhaps you would like to start writing your own psalms, prayers, or poems to God. Keeping a spiritual journal of your thoughts and feelings for the Lord, for others, and for yourself might be a first step. Ronald Klug provides this helpful guidance for getting started: "There are no rules for keeping a spiritual journal. Your way is the right way."[6]

You might want to continue reading through the Psalms, studying the different topics and themes you find in them. Choose parts or whole psalms to memorize so that your meditation will be rich and meaningful. As this discipline becomes a part of your life, how exciting it will be to look back and realize a growing intimacy with the Creator who has become your Confidant.

Notes

Preface
1. Charles H. Spurgeon, *The Treasury of David* (McLean, VA: MacDonald Publishing Co., n.d.), vol.1, preface to part 2.

Introduction to Part One — The Desire for Intimacy
1. Dan Allender, in *IBC Perspective: A Publication of the Institute of Biblical Counseling*, ed. Lawrence J. Crabb, Jr. (Winona Lake, IN, 1985), vol. 1, no. 1, p. 27.

Chapter 1 — Our Longing for Intimacy
1. From the hymn "What a Friend We Have in Jesus," lyrics by Joseph M. Scriven, in *Hymns for the Family of God* (Nashville: Paragon, 1976), #466.
2. A. W. Tozer, *The Pursuit of God* (Harrisburg, PA: Christian Publications, n.d.), p. 15.
3. J. Oswald Sanders, *Enjoying Intimacy with God* (Chicago: Moody Press, 1980), p. 20.
4. Charles H. Spurgeon, *The Treasury of David* (McLean, VA: MacDonald Publishing Co., n.d.), vol. 2, p. 253.
5. Thomas Pierson, in Spurgeon, vol. 3, part 2, p. 343.
6. Spurgeon, p. 463.

Chapter 2 — God's Desire for Us
1. From the hymn "The Wonder of It All," lyrics by George Beverly Shea, in *Hymns for the Family of God* (Nashville: Paragon, 1976), #13.
2. J. I. Packer, *Knowing God* (Downers Grove, IL: InterVarsity Press, 1979), p. 37.
3. Charles H. Spurgeon, *The Treasury of David* (McLean, VA: MacDonald Publishing Co., n.d.), vol. 1, p. 354.
4. Quoted in Spurgeon, vol. 1, p. 89.
5. C. S. Lewis, *The Four Loves* (New York: Harcourt, Brace & Co., 1960), pp. 126-127.

Chapter 3 — God Is Righteous
1. From the hymn "The Solid Rock," lyrics by Edward Mote, in *Hymns for the Family of God* (Nashville: Paragon, 1976), #92.
2. A. W. Tozer, *The Knowledge of the Holy* (New York: Harper & Row, 1961), p. 92.
3. Sinclair Ferguson, *Kingdom Life in a Fallen World* (Colorado Springs, CO: NavPress, 1986), pp. 45-46.
4. Albert Barnes, *Notes on the Old Testament: Psalms* (Grand Rapids, MI: Baker, 1998), p. 79.

5. Eugene Peterson, *A Long Obedience in the Same Direction* (Downers Grove, IL: InterVarsity Press, 1980), pp. 128-129.
6. Charles H. Spurgeon, *The Treasury of David* (McLean, VA: MacDonald Publishing Co., n.d.), vol. 2, part 2, p. 436.
7. Ray Stedman, *Folk Songs of Faith*, from the *Bible Commentary for Laymen* series (Glendale, CA: Gospel Light Publications, 1973), p. 47.

Chapter 4 — God Is Trustworthy
1. From the hymn "'Tis So Sweet to Trust in Jesus," lyrics by Louisa M. R. Stead, in *Hymns for the Family of God* (Nashville: Paragon, 1976), #91.
2. George Mueller, in *Streams in the Desert*, comp. Mrs. Charles E. Cowman (Minneapolis, MN: Worldwide Publications, 1979), pp. 19-20.
3. Sir Richard Baker, in Charles H. Spurgeon, *The Treasury of David* (McLean, VA: MacDonald Publishing Co., n.d.), vol. 2, p. 446.
4. Spurgeon, vol. 1, p. 465.
5. John Calvin, in Spurgeon, vol. 1, part 2, p. 72.
6. A. W. Tozer, *The Knowledge of the Holy* (New York: Harper & Row, 1961), p. 70.

Chapter 5 — God Is a Refuge
1. From the hymn "Hiding in Thee," lyrics by William O. Cushing, in *Hymns for the Family of God* (Nashville: Paragon, 1976), #70.
2. *The New Bible Commentary*, ed. Donald Guthrie (Grand Rapids, MI: Eerdmans, n.d.), p. 508.
3. Eugene Peterson, *Earth and Altar* (Downers Grove, IL: InterVarsity, 1985), pp. 72-73.
4. Charles H. Spurgeon, *The Treasury of David* (McLean, VA: MacDonald Publishing Co., n.d.), vol. 2, p. 89.
5. Amy Carmichael, *His Thoughts Said . . . His Father Said . . .* (Ft. Washington, PA: Christian Literature Crusade, 1941), #113.

Chapter 6 — God Is Responsive
1. From the hymn "For Those Tears I Died," lyrics by Marsha Stevens, in *Hymns for the Family of God* (Nashville: Paragon, 1976), #436.
2. R. Tuck, in *The Pulpit Commentary*, ed. H. D. M. Spence and Joseph S. Excell (Peabody, MA: Hendrickson Publishers, n.d.), vol. 8, Book 5, p. 77.
3. *The New Bible Commentary*, ed. Donald Guthrie (Grand Rapids, MI: Eerdmans, n.d.), p. 506.
4. Albert Barnes, *Notes on the Old Testament: Psalms* (Grand Rapids, MI: Baker, 1998), p. 295.
5. William Blake, in Tuck, vol. 8, p. 77.

Introduction to Part Three — The Essentials of Intimacy
1. Jerry Bridges, *The Practice of Godliness* (Colorado Springs, CO: NavPress, 1983), p. 29.
2. Derek Kidner, *Tyndale Old Testament Commentaries: Psalms 1–72*, gen. ed. D. J. Wiseman (Downers Grove, IL: InterVarsity, 1973), p. 157.

Chapter 7—Reverence for God

1. From the hymn "O Worship the King," lyrics by Robert Grant, in *Hymns for the Family of God* (Nashville: Paragon, 1976), #336.
2. John White, *Daring to Draw Near* (Downers Grove, IL: InterVarsity, 1977), pp. 99-100.
3. A. F. Kirkpatrick, *The Book of Psalms* (Grand Rapids, MI: Baker, 1982), p. 817.
4. Eugene Peterson, *A Long Obedience in the Same Direction* (Downers Grove, IL: InterVarsity Press, 1980), p. 116.
5. R. Tuck, in *The Pulpit Commentary*, ed. H. D. M. Spence and Joseph S. Excell (Peabody, MA: Hendrickson Publishers, n.d.), vol. 8, book 5, p. 42.
6. Robert Nisbet, in Charles Haddon Spurgeon, *Psalms*, ed. David Otis Fuller (Grand Rapids, MI: Kregel, 1968), p. 594.

Chapter 8—Truthfulness with God

1. From the hymn "I Must Tell Jesus," lyrics by Elisha A. Hoffman, in *Hymns for the Family of God* (Nashville: Paragon, 1976), #49.
2. Warren Wiersbe, *Meet Yourself in the Psalms* (Wheaton, IL: Victor, 1983), p. 21.
3. Abraham Wright, in Charles Haddon Spurgeon, *Psalms*, ed. David Otis Fuller (Grand Rapids, MI: Kregel, 1968), p. 654.
4. Charles H. Spurgeon, *The Treasury of David* (McLean, VA: MacDonald Publishing Co., n.d.), vol. 1, part 2, p. 401.
5. Tim Stafford, *Knowing the Face of God* (Grand Rapids, MI: Zondervan, 1986), p. 134.

Chapter 9—Love for God's Word

1. From the hymn "How Firm a Foundation," in *Hymns for the Family of God* (Nashville: Paragon, 1976), #32.
2. Charles Haddon Spurgeon, *Psalms*, ed. David Otis Fuller (Grand Rapids, MI: Kregel, 1968), p. 511.
3. Spurgeon, pp. 510-511.
4. Spurgeon, p. 519.
5. A. F. Kirkpatrick, *The Book of Psalms* (Grand Rapids, MI: Baker, 1982), p. 701.
6. Matthew Henry, as quoted in Spurgeon, p. 510.

Chapter 10—The Growth of Intimacy

1. From the hymn "It Is Well with My Soul," lyrics by Horatio G. Spafford, in *Hymns for the Family of God* (Nashville: Paragon, 1976), #495.
2. Carlo Carretto, in *A Guide to Prayer for Ministers and Other Servants*, by Reuben P. Job and Norman Sawchuck (Nashville, TN: Upper Room, 1983), p. 15.
3. J. Oswald Sanders, *Enjoying Intimacy with God* (Chicago: Moody Press, 1980), p. 66.
4. Saint Anselm, in Charles Haddon Spurgeon, *Psalms*, ed. David Otis Fuller (Grand Rapids, MI: Kregel, 1968), p. 605.

Chapter 11—Praise: The Expression of Intimacy

1. From the hymn "O for a Thousand Tongues to Sing," lyrics by Charles Wesley, in *Hymns for the Family of God* (Nashville: Paragon, 1976), #349.

2. Josh McDowell and Dale Bellis, *Evidence for Joy* (Waco, TX: Word, 1984), pp. 107-108.
3. Charles Haddon Spurgeon, *Psalms,* ed. David Otis Fuller (Grand Rapids, MI: Kregel, 1968), p. 404.
4. C. S. Lewis, *Reflections on the Psalms* (San Diego: Harcourt Brace Jovanovich, 1958), p. 95.
5. Alexander Maclaren, quoted in A. F. Kirkpatrick, *The Book of Psalms* (Grand Rapids, MI: Baker, 1982), pp. 831-832.

Chapter 12 — A Life of Deepening Intimacy
1. From the hymn "More Love to Thee, O Christ," lyrics by William H. Doane, in *Hymns for the Family of God* (Nashville: Paragon, 1976), #476.
2. J. Oswald Sanders, *Enjoying Intimacy with God* (Chicago: Moody Press, 1980), p. 20.
3. Roger C. Palms, *The Pleasure of His Company: How to Be a Friend of God* (Wheaton, IL: Tyndale, 1982), p. 66.
4. A. W. Tozer, *The Pursuit of God* (Harrisburg, PA: Christian Publications, n.d.), p. 17.
5. C. Donald Cole, *Thirsting for God* (Westchester, IL: Crossway Books, 1986), p. 298.
6. Ronald Klug, *How to Keep a Spiritual Journal* (Nashville, TN: Nelson, 1982), p. 58.

About the Author

CYNTHIA HEALD is an author and speaker known to many women through her best-selling Bible studies and books, including *Becoming a Woman of Excellence,* which has sold over 6 million copies since its initial publication in 1986.

A native Texan, Heald graduated from the University of Texas with a B.A. in English. She and her husband, Jack, a veterinarian by profession, are on full-time staff with The Navigators. They have four grown children and six grandchildren and reside in Tucson, Arizona.

IF YOU ENJOYED THIS BOOK BY CYNTHIA HEALD, YOU'LL WANT TO EXPERIENCE HER ADDITIONAL TITLES INCLUDING...

Becoming a Woman of Excellence

Becoming a Woman of Freedom

Becoming a Woman of Purpose

Becoming a Woman of Prayer

Loving Your Husband

Loving Your Wife (with Jack Heald)

Walking Together (with Jack Heald)

Abiding in Christ

Get your copies today at your local bookstore, visit our website at www.navpress.com, or call (800) 366-7788 and ask for a FREE catalog of NavPress products.

NAVPRESS
BRINGING TRUTH TO LIFE
www.navpress.com